Soft Skills Sleuths

I0896422

LEADERSHIP

Investigating Life Skills Success

Diane Lindsey Reeves with Connie Hansen
Illustrations by Ruth Bennett

Cherry Lake Press

Published in the United States of America by Cherry Lake Publishing Group
Ann Arbor, Michigan
www.cherrylakepublishing.com

Created and produced by Bright Futures Press
www.brightfuturespress.com

Reading Advisor: Marla Conn, MS, Ed., Literacy specialist, Read-Ability, Inc.
Illustrator: Ruth Bennett
Cover and Page Designer: Kathy Heming
Design Elements: © mijatmijatovic/Shutterstock.com; © GoodStudio/Shutterstock.com; © Denis Cristo/Shutterstock.com; © Lorelyn Medina/Shutterstock.com; © Yaroshenko Olena/Shutterstock.com; © rangsan paidaen/Shutterstock.com

Copyright ©2021 by Cherry Lake Publishing Group
All rights reserved. No part of this book may be reproduced or utilized in any form or by any means without written permission from the publisher.

Cherry Lake Press is an imprint of Cherry Lake Publishing Group.

Library of Congress Cataloging-in-Publication Data has been filed and is available at catalog.loc.gov

Cherry Lake Publishing Group would like to acknowledge the work of the Partnership for 21st Century Learning, a Network of Battelle for Kids. Please visit http://www.battelleforkids.org/networks/p21 for more information.

Printed in the United States of America
Corporate Graphics

TABLE OF CONTENTS

What Are Soft Skills and

Skills are needed to succeed at any job you can imagine. Different jobs require different skills. Professional baseball players need good batting and catching skills. Brain surgeons need steady hands and lots of practice with a scalpel. These are examples of **hard skills** necessary to do specific jobs.

Everyone needs "**soft skills**" to succeed in life. Soft skills get personal. They are about how you behave and treat people. Soft skills are the skills you need to be the very best *you* at home, work, and school.

"Sounds good," you say. "But I don't have a job. Why do I need to worry about soft skills?"

Ahh, but you do have a job. In fact, you have a very important job. You are a student, and your job is to learn as much as you can. Learning soft skills makes you a better student now. It also gets you ready to succeed in any career you choose later.

Leadership is a highly prized soft skill. Leadership is the ability to motivate people to work together to achieve a common goal. It is needed in schools and sports teams as well as in business and politics. Becoming a good leader isn't easy. It is something that can be learned with practice and by following good examples.

In this book, you get to be a soft skills **sleuth**. You will track down clues about what good (and not so good!) leadership looks like. You will **investigate** four soft skills every good leader needs:

- **Savvy**
- **Integrity**
- **Inclusivity**
- **Influence**

Why Do I Need Them?

HOW TO USE THIS BOOK

Here's how you can be a soft skills sleuth. In each chapter:

- **Gather the facts.** Read the description about the soft skill.
- **Read the case file.** Check out a situation where soft skills are needed.
- **Investigate the case.** Look for clues showing soft skills *successes* and soft skills *mistakes*. Keep track of the clues on a blank sheet of paper.
- **Crack the case.** Did you spot all the clues?

SOFT SKILL #1

The word **savvy** means having common sense and good judgment. It is used to describe leaders in a couple of ways. A savvy leader is one who is smart, well-informed, and successful in navigating life. This type of leader is said to have "street smarts."

A socially savvy leader is one who has good people skills. That means they like being with people, and, for the most part, people like being with them. They are well-mannered and can handle themselves in social situations. Aspiring young leaders like you can be fun and friendly in the cafeteria. But you also know how to behave while enjoying a school concert or play.

Successful leaders are both street and socially savvy. Leaders lead people. People look for positive character traits in their leaders. They respond well to kindness, honesty, and a good attitude. They listen when a leader communicates in a friendly, clear, and inclusive way. They accept hard decisions when they know they can trust a leader to be fair.

Here's the deal: you can't be a leader unless other people want to follow you. A savvy leader is one whom others admire and look up to. This is true for the adults who lead big companies. It is also true for students who lead clubs, sports teams, and student government.

Hone Your People Skills

- Make it easy for others to like you by being kind and friendly.
- Keep a positive outlook and encourage others to do the same.
- Handle conflict fairly and without playing favorites.
- Show interest in other people and their ideas.

"Leaders must be close enough to relate to others, but far enough ahead to motivate them."
—John C. Maxwell

SAVVY

SOFT SKILLS CASE #1: SAVVY

It's time to elect a new class president. Students count on their class president to do a good job. It is clear that some candidates are both street and socially savvy. They are prepared and greeting the voters. Their people skills are winning votes. Other candidates will probably end up a few votes short in the ballot box.

Which candidates would you vote for?

DO: Investigate savvy successes and mistakes!

DO NOT: Write in this book!

It is school election day! Which candidates are winning the votes with their savvy leadership skills?

A VOTE FOR SAVVY LEADERSHIP

SAVVY

The votes are in! Which candidates win for showing strong savvy skills?

Did you find all the successes and MISTAKES?

Start here!

Success.
Well-prepared and friendly gets the votes.

Success.
Shaking hands shows you care.

Mistake.
Trading sodas instead of ideas for votes?

CASE NOTES

Are your street smarts showing?

Mistake. Vote for me or not, I don't really care.

Success. Team Lisa leads the way!

Did you find them all?

Mistake. Cell phones don't vote but ignored voters do. Too bad it won't be for you.

Mistake. Yes. No. Maybe so. Wishy-washy whiplash!

Mistake. Disorganized, disrespectful, and clueless. Can you spot all three?

SOFT SKILL #2

One of the nicest things you can say about someone is that they have **integrity**. To have integrity means a person is known for being honest and having high moral standards. In other words, you can count on a person of integrity to be the real deal. They are good people who will do their best not to let you down.

Kind, generous, trustworthy, helpful, genuine—when you see these traits in a person, you know they have integrity. No, they aren't perfect. But people with integrity admit their mistakes and work hard to solve problems.

Courage is another sign of integrity. Life is complicated, even when you are young. A person with integrity has strong beliefs about what is right and wrong. This person stands up for those **principles**, even if they aren't popular or easy.

For instance, suppose you went to the store to buy some candy. The candy costs $2 and you give the cashier $10. The cashier owes you $8 in change but gives you $18 instead. That's $10 more! It isn't your fault that the cashier made a mistake. It would be easy to pocket that cash. But you value the principle of honesty. You show integrity by returning the extra money. You will feel better about your decision, and so will the cashier!

Let Your Integrity Shine

- Keep your promises.
- Learn from your mistakes.
- Find the good in other people.
- Hang out with good people.
- Be willing to lend a hand when someone needs help.
- Treat people with respect.

"Real integrity is doing the right thing, knowing that nobody's going to know whether you did it or not."
—Oprah Winfrey

INTEGRITY

SOFT SKILLS CASE #2: INTEGRITY

On your mark, get set, GO!

Today is the fun run—and, whew, is it hot! As everyone dashes to the finish line, their integrity is put to the test. Some runners are just out for themselves. Others are putting others first. Which students are leading the way?

DO:
Investigate integrity successes and mistakes!

DO NOT:
Write in this book!

EXCUSE ME, YOUR INTEGRITY IS SHOWING

It's a race to the finish line of integrity. Who wins the race? Those with integrity or those in it only for the win?

FINISH
HYDRATE!!!

INTEGRITY

Crossing the finish line first isn't the only way to be a winner. Where do you see signs of integrity?

Did you find all the successes and MISTAKES?

Start here!

Mistake.
Taking a shortcut to the finish line, are you?

Success!
Let's finish the race together.

Mistake.
Making fun of other people is a losing move.

Success!
Come on! You can do it!

Success!
Let me help you cool off.

CASE NOTES

Count on integrity to win the race!

Mistake.
It's a foot race, not a bike race.

Did you find them all?

Success!
You look thirsty. Have a drink.

Mistake.
Out of my way! I want to win.

Mistake.
All this water is mine, mine, mine.

SOFT SKILL #3

People come in all sizes, ages, and colors. They come from different places and have different beliefs. Their abilities, skills, and interests are not the same. It is important to understand that all people are created equal. But all people are not the same.

This variety, or **diversity**, makes the world more interesting. It also makes it more challenging as everyone figures out how to get along with others.

Sometimes **stereotypes** get in the way of **inclusivity**. People might believe that everyone from a specific culture or lifestyle thinks and acts a certain way. Have you ever heard something described as being "as American as baseball, hot dogs, and apple pie"? Those things may be part of American culture. But it is a stereotype to think that every American likes them in the same way.

The same is true when you encounter people from different races, backgrounds, and cultures. You may automatically assume that you know certain things about them. But when you get acquainted, you are likely to be surprised. Sure, there are interesting differences about their experiences. It is important to respect those differences. However, as human beings existing together on Planet Earth, you have much in common too.

Being inclusive means that everyone is welcome. Everyone gets the same chance to belong as you do. Strong leaders choose inclusivity!

Small Steps Toward Inclusivity

- Choose to include others who aren't like you.
- Be careful not to judge other people by the way they look.
- Be friendly to all the students at your school.

"A diverse mix of voices leads to better discussions, decisions, and outcomes for everyone."
—Sundar Pichai

INCLUSIVITY

SOFT SKILLS CASE #3: INCLUSIVITY

Let's play ball! It's the blue team against the red team. Everyone wants to play, and everyone wants to win. But most of all, everyone wants to have fun. No one wants to be left out.

The team captains pick their players. Which team is being inclusive of all the students?

DO:
Investigate inclusivity successes and mistakes!

DO NOT:
Write in this book!

Which team is making everyone feel welcome? Which team is choosing only players who are like themselves?

PUT OUT THE WELCOME MAT

INCLUSIVITY

Which team is diverse? Which one is leaving out people who are different from them?

Did you **find** all the successes *and* **MISTAKES?**

Start here!

Mistake.
Winning is more important than people.

Success!
All abilities welcome.

Mistake.
No girls allowed?

CASE NOTES

Success! Short, tall, little, big.

Mistake. Words can hurt.

One for all and all for one!

Did you find them all?

Mistake. Saying nothing means you say something is okay.

Success! The team's all here. Let's play ball!

Mistake. Star athletes only.

SOFT SKILL #4

Learning how to **influence** people is a lot like learning to make a new friend. It all starts with making a good impression. The best way to make a good impression is to be a good person. This is where character counts. Are you friendly and kind? Do you respect other people? Can people count on you to be honest and fair?

An influential person is someone who shapes how people act or how events come together. Influential people are sometimes called "movers and shakers." That's because they know how to make things happen. Influencers **motivate** people to support specific ideas and inspire them to take action. Successful politicians are influential people. They rally people around various beliefs or causes and inspire them to vote.

Influential people are not bossy people. They do not force people to do what they want. They build connections and lead by example. Sports team captains do this all the time. Captains use their influence to help the team reach their common goal: winning!

Of course, influence can go both ways. Maybe you've been warned to stay away from someone who is a "bad influence." That person might try to encourage you to do the wrong thing. The best leaders use their influence in good ways.

How to Be an Influential Friend

- Believe in yourself.
- Mind your manners.
- Make other people feel important.
- Admit your mistakes.
- Lend a helping hand.

INFLUENCE

SOFT SKILLS CASE #4: INFLUENCE

Field trip! All the students get to vote on where they want to go for the end-of-the-year field trip. There are three choices: the zoo, the amusement park, and the aquarium. There are leaders for each choice, and it's their job to influence the students to choose their trip.

Turn the page to catch all the action. Which leaders are having the most influence?

DO:
Investigate influence successes and mistakes!

DO NOT:
Write in this book!

LET'S TAKE A FIELD TRIP!

Three great choices, but only one will win. How are these leaders influencing their classmates?

INFLUENCE

Which field trip would you choose? What influenced your decision?

Did you find all the successes and MISTAKES?

Start here!

Success!
A friendly smile says "Hello! You are welcome to join us."

Success!
Knowing your stuff and sharing it in creative ways.

Mistake.
Criticizing other trips doesn't make yours better.

CASE NOTES

How can you make friends and influence people?

Success! Welcoming everyone to join in the fun.

Mistake. Forcing people to go have fun.

Did you find them all?

Mistake. If you don't care about your own field trip, who will?

Success! Fishing for votes with great information and prizes.

Mistake. Making false claims is a bad look.

WHAT HAVE YOU Learned?

LEADERSHIP QUIZ

Question 1:

To be ____________ means to show common sense and good judgment.

Question 2:

Socially savvy leaders have good ____________ skills.

Question 3:

People with ____________ have high moral standards.

Question 4:

A ____________ is a strong belief about something that is right or wrong.

Question 5:

Thinking that all Americans like to eat hot dogs is an example of a ____________.

Question 6:

____________ means that everyone is welcome.

Question 7:

Different genders, races, and backgrounds are examples of ____________.

Question 8:

Influential people know how to ____________ others to act in certain ways.

ANSWERS

1. *savvy*
2. *people*
3. *integrity*
4. *principle*
5. *stereotype*
6. *Inclusivity or Inclusive*
7. *diversity*
8. *motivate or inspire*

Leadership soft skills start here!

GLOSSARY

diversity (dih-VUR-sih-tee) everything that makes people different from each other

hard skills (HAHRD SKILZ) specific skills needed to do a specific job

inclusivity (in-kloo-SIV-ih-tee) the practice of welcoming everyone, especially those who might be left out, such as those who have physical or mental disabilities and members of minority groups

influence (IN-floo-uhns) to have an effect on or have the power to change someone

integrity (in-TEG-rih-tee) the quality of being honest and having high moral principles

investigate (in-VES-tih-gate) to gather information or clues about something

motivate (MOH-tuh-vate) to inspire someone to act

principles (PRIN-suh-puhlz) basic truths, laws, or beliefs

savvy (SAHV-ee) practical knowledge and ability; experienced and well-informed

sleuth (SLOOTH) a detective, or person who is good at finding facts and clues

soft skills (SAWFT SKILZ) behaviors and personality traits people use every day to succeed in life

stereotypes (STER-ee-oh-tipes) widely held but overly simple ideas, opinions, or images of a person, group, or thing

INDEX

ABOUT THE AUTHORS

Diane Lindsey Reeves likes to write books that help students figure out what they want to be when they grow up. She mostly lives in Washington, D.C., but spends as much time as she can in North Carolina and South Carolina with her grandkids.

Connie Hansen spent 25 years teaching college students about successful life skills. She lives in Lynchburg, Virginia where her favorite thing to do is play with her grandchildren. Her happy place is the beach!

ABOUT THE ILLUSTRATOR

Ruth Bennett lives in a small country village in the heart of Norfolk, England, with her two cats, Queen Elizabeth and Queen Victoria. She loves petting dogs, watching movies, and drawing, of course!